WORLD EXPLORERS

Voyages to the Indies

1400–1520s

Danny Miller

PICTURE CREDITS

Cover (back) Private Collection/Heini Schneebeli/Bridgeman Art Library; cover art Todd Leonardo; cover (top right), page 17 (bottom) Bob Krist/Corbis; page 1 Bruce Dale/National Geographic Image Collection; page 2 British Museum, London, UK/Bridgeman Art Library; pages 3 (top left), 4 (bottom), 8 (bottom left) Scala/Art Resource, NY; page 3 (bottom) Giraudon/Bridgeman Art Library; pages 4 (top left), 17 (top) Bojan Brecelj/Corbis; page 5 (top) Anthony Blake Photo Library; pages 5 (bottom left), 10 (right), 18 AKG Images; page 5 (bottom middle) The Pierpont Morgan Library Ms. M.525, f.45v/Art Resource, NY; page 5 (bottom right) Dinodia Picture Agency, Bombay, India/Bridgeman Art Library; pages 6 (left), 13 (top right) Mary Evans Picture Library; pages 6–7 Historical Picture Archive/Corbis; pages 8 (top left), 12 Charles O'Rear/Corbis; pages 8 (bottom right), 27 Tony Arruza/Corbis; pages 10 (bottom left), 11 (top left) Dennis Blachut/Corbis; page 11 (right) Michael Holford; pages 13 (bottom left), 30 (bottom left) Photodisc; pages 13, 32 (bottom right) Archivo Iconografico, S.A./Corbis; pages 15 (top left), 20 Ancient Art and Architecture Collection; page 14 (bottom left) Private Collection/Index/Bridgeman Art Library; page 14 (bottom right) Giraudon/Art Resource, NY; page 16 Wolfgang Kaehler/Corbis; page 19 Burstein Collection/Corbis; page 21 Werner Forman/Art Resource, NY; pages 22 (top left), 26 Michael S. Yamashita/Corbis; page 22 (bottom left) The Art Archive, Maine Museum Lisbon/Dagli Orti; pages 22 (bottom right), 24, 28 (bottom left) Bjorn Landstrom/National Geographic Image Collection; page 25 (left) Galen Rowell/Corbis; page 25 (right) Detail from the frontispiece to *A Voyage round the World in his Majesty's ship the Dolphin commanded by the Hon. Comm. Byron* 1767; pages 28 (right), 30 (top left) Erich Lessing/Art Resource, NY; page 29 British Library, London, UK/Bridgeman Art Library; page 31 Victoria & Albert Museum, London/Art Resource, NY.

Produced through the worldwide resources of the National Geographic Society, John M. Fahey, Jr., President and Chief Executive Officer; Gilbert M. Grosvenor, Chairman of the Board; Nina D. Hoffman, Executive Vice President and President, Books and Education Publishing Group.

PREPARED BY NATIONAL GEOGRAPHIC SCHOOL PUBLISHING
Ericka Markman, Senior Vice President and President, Children's Books and Education Publishing Group; Steve Mico, Vice President, Editorial Director; Marianne Hiland, Executive Editor; Anita Schwartz, Project Editor; Jim Hiscott, Design Manager; Kristin Hanneman, Illustrations Manager; Diana Bourdrez, Picture Editor; Matt Wascavage, Manager of Publishing Services; Sean Philpotts, Production Manager.

MANUFACTURING AND QUALITY MANAGEMENT
Christopher A. Liedel, Chief Financial Officer; Phillip L. Schlosser, Director; Clifton M. Brown, Manager.

ART DIRECTION Dan Banks, Project Design Company

CONSULTANT/REVIEWER
Dr. Margit E. McGuire, School of Education, Seattle University, Seattle, Washington

BOOK DEVELOPMENT Nieman Inc.

BOOK DESIGN Three Communication Design, LLC

PICTURE EDITING AND MANAGEMENT
Corrine L. Brock
In the Lupe, Inc.

MAP DEVELOPMENT AND PRODUCTION Elizabeth Wolf

Published by the National Geographic Society
1145 17th Street, N.W.
Washington, D.C. 20036-4688

ISBN: 0-7922-4543-1

Printed in Canada

cover (top right): Whole nutmegs

cover: Fleet of carracks

page 1: First globe to show Magellan's route around the world

page 2: African mask fringed with figures of Portuguese soldiers

page 3 (top): An astrolabe, used to plot a ship's path

page 3 (bottom): Caravel

Table of Contents

───────── ✳ ─────────

The World in 1400

In 1400, some of the most valuable trade goods in the world were spices, such as pepper, nutmeg, and cloves. These spices came from faraway lands in Asia known as the **Indies**. Europeans used spices for medicines and to keep meat from rotting.

Spices reached Europe by a long route through the **Near East**. This made them very costly. There were also wars between the Christians of Europe and the people of the Near East, who were **Muslims**. These wars stopped the flow of spices.

The spice trade made cities like Genoa, Italy, rich.

In 1400, people in Europe were not sure what many parts of the world looked like. Their maps showed the Indian Ocean with land on all sides of it. If that were true, it would make it impossible to sail around Africa to India. There was only one way to find out for sure—try to sail there.

Portugal is a small country on the southwest coast of Europe. The Portuguese wanted to find a sea route around Africa to the Indies. The problem was that sailors were afraid to go very far down the African coast. They believed there was a boiling sea full of monsters there.

Around 1420, a Portuguese prince, Henry the Navigator, founded a school for sailors. He began a search for a route to the Indies. Over the next 100 years, this search would involve many great explorers, including Bartholomeu Dias, Vasco da Gama, and Ferdinand Magellan.

Voyage of Bartholomeu Dias

Voyage of Christopher Columbus

Founding of Prince Henry's school

Voyage of Vasco da Gama

Voyage of Ferdinand Magellan

1400   1425   1450   1475   1500   1525

To explore new routes to the Indies, Portugal needed new types of ships. The ships had to be strong, fast, and easy to handle. The Arabs used boats with large, three-sided sails called **lateens**. These boats were swift and sturdy, and they handled well.

The Portuguese developed a new type of ship called a **caravel** based on the Arab boats. The caravel was a small ship, about 75 feet (23 meters) long. It could hold supplies for a crew of about 20 men. Caravels were well-suited for Portugal's first short voyages of exploration down the western coast of Africa.

The Portuguese later developed a larger ship called a **carrack** for longer voyages across the open sea. Carracks used both lateens and square-rigged sails. The carrack was about 50 feet (15 meters) longer than the caravel. Because the carrack was larger, it could carry much larger loads of supplies than the caravel. Carracks were also strong enough to carry cannons. Exploration was a risky business.

Carrack

Caravel

spare ropes

spare sails

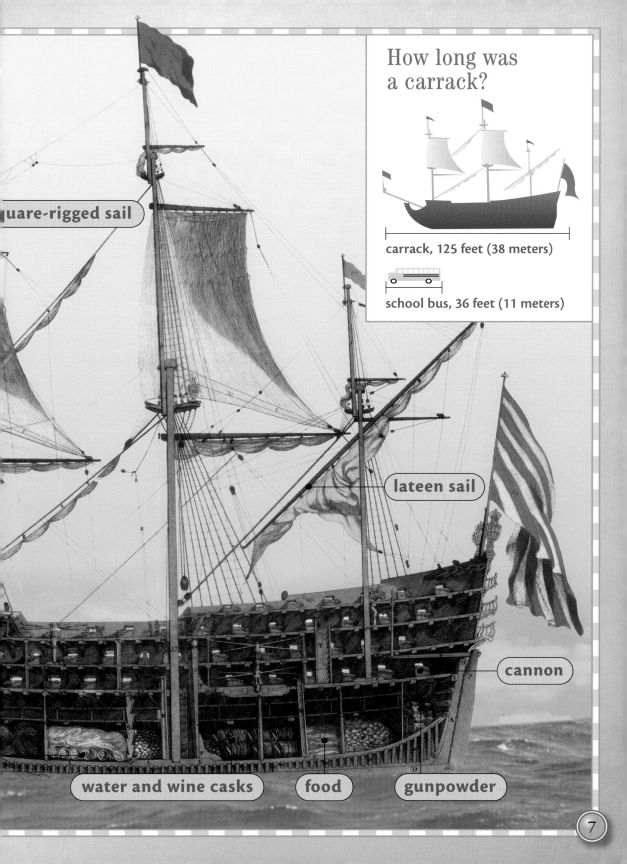

How long was a carrack?

carrack, 125 feet (38 meters)

school bus, 36 feet (11 meters)

square-rigged sail

lateen sail

cannon

water and wine casks

food

gunpowder

Chapter 1

Prince Henry the Navigator

Why did a small country like Portugal become so important in the history of exploration? It all began with a prince who is known in history as Henry the Navigator. A **navigator** is a person skilled at plotting a ship's path.

Prince Henry was a son of the king of Portugal. Even as a child, Henry was interested in the sea. When he was 21, Prince Henry led troops against a Muslim city in North Africa. When he took the city, he found a treasure of gold, silver, and spices.

Prince Henry

Sagres today

Prince Henry's World
Bartholomeu Dias's Route, 1487-1488

Lisbon · PORTUGAL
Sagres
Madeira Islands
Canary Islands
Cape Bojador
AFRICA
Equator
ATLANTIC OCEAN
INDIAN OCEAN
Cape of Good Hope

Kilometers
0   1000   2000
Miles
0   1000   2000

Prince Henry knew that this wealth came from the Indies. How could Portugal find a new route there? Was there a way to sail around Africa? How could he find out? In 1419, he moved to Sagres (SAH–gres), at the southwest tip of Portugal. Staring out into the Atlantic Ocean, he dreamed of great voyages of exploration.

At Sagres, Prince Henry gathered the best scholars and sailors. His experts shared their knowledge to help Portugal find a new route to the riches of the Indies. In this way, he began the world's first school of navigation. Although Prince Henry himself never sailed on any of the voyages to come, he started a new Age of Discovery.

Beyond the Green Sea of Darkness

Even with better ships, Prince Henry had a hard time finding people who were willing to sail down the coast of Africa. Most sailors thought that beyond Cape Bojador (BOH–hah–dor) on the African coast was the deadly Green Sea of Darkness. Sailors believed that the water there was boiling hot and full of monsters.

For 12 long years, Prince Henry sent out ship after ship with orders to sail past Cape Bojador. His crews went farther south than any Europeans had ever been. They found small islands in the waters off Africa, such as Madeira and the Canary Islands. But every time they got near Cape Bojador, the sailors would panic and demand to go back.

Sailors feared monsters would attack their ships beyond Cape Bojador. ▶

Finally, in 1434, a brave Portuguese captain sailed past the cape. And guess what? The water didn't boil! The ship didn't burst into flames! There were no horrible monsters! This voyage put an end to the fearful stories of the Green Sea of Darkness.

Little by little, Prince Henry's ships made their way down the African coast. The Portuguese now came in contact with African peoples. They found that they could make money by capturing Africans and selling them as slaves.

Prince Henry did nothing to stop this. He needed the money for his ships. Also, the Africans weren't Christians. Europeans believed it was all right to enslave Africans if they could convert them to the "true faith." Some African villages fought back, but the kidnappings continued. The slave trade was making some Portuguese rich.

Across Cultures

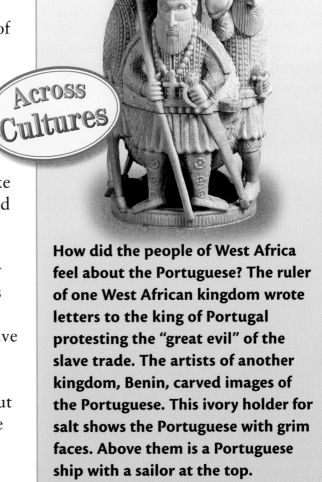

How did the people of West Africa feel about the Portuguese? The ruler of one West African kingdom wrote letters to the king of Portugal protesting the "great evil" of the slave trade. The artists of another kingdom, Benin, carved images of the Portuguese. This ivory holder for salt shows the Portuguese with grim faces. Above them is a Portuguese ship with a sailor at the top.

The Endless Coast

When Prince Henry died in 1460, his sailors had still not found a new route to the Indies. But the voyages of exploration continued after his death. The Portuguese ships traveled another 1,500 miles (2,400 kilometers). Still there was no sign of the end of the African continent. Meanwhile, there was a lot of money to be made from the trade in African slaves, ivory, and gold.

In 1487, an explorer named Bartholomeu Dias set sail with two caravels and a store ship with food and supplies. He was determined to find the tip of Africa. The farther he went down the coast, the rougher the waters became. After two weeks of storms, the two caravels were still afloat, but the store ship was gone. What should Dias do?

◄ The Cape of Good Hope is at Africa's southern tip.

Prester John's subjects kneel in front of him. ▶

His sailors wanted to turn back, but Dias pushed on. On February 3, 1488, the Portuguese finally saw land—to the north! They had sailed right past the southern tip of Africa. One of Prince Henry's dreams had been realized, almost 30 years after his death.

When Dias returned to Portugal in December 1488, the king was overjoyed by the news. Dias had named the tip of Africa the Cape of Storms. But the king renamed it the Cape of Good Hope. The door was now open for Portugal to chart a new trade route to the Indies.

Elephant tusks were the source of Africa's ivory.

?
It's a Mystery

Prester John

One of Prince Henry's goals was to find a mysterious Christian king named Prester John, or "John the Priest." Legend said that Prester John's country was somewhere in Africa. It was full of gold and precious stones. Prince Henry hoped Prester John would help Portugal fight the Muslims. Portuguese explorers searched long for Prester John's mysterious kingdom. They never found it.

Chapter 2

Vasco da Gama

On July 8, 1497, a small Portuguese fleet set sail for the Indies. It included a caravel, two carracks, and a large store ship. There were enough supplies for three years at sea. The ships were loaded with food and water.

There were extra sails and anchors, gifts for the people the crew would meet on the trip, and plenty of weapons and ammunition. The fleet's commander, Vasco da Gama, was a skillful sailor and brave soldier.

The fleet of Vasco da Gama (left) set sail from the harbor of Lisbon, Portugal's capital (above).

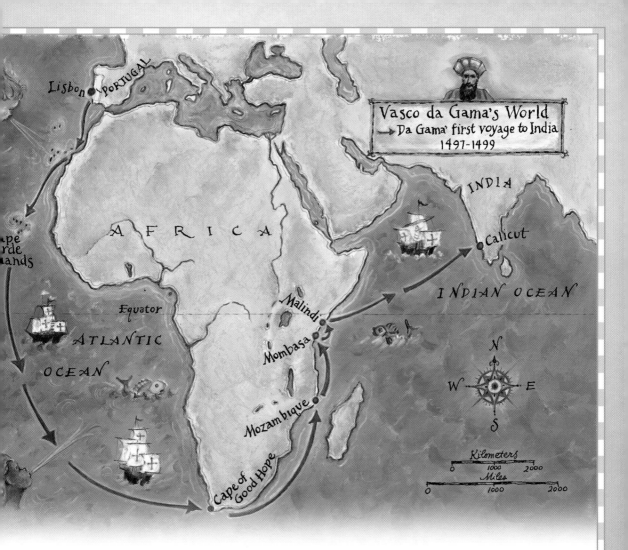

Vasco da Gama's World
→ Da Gama' first voyage to India
1497-1499

Lisbon PORTUGAL

INDIA

Cape Verde Islands

AFRICA

Calicut

Equator

INDIAN OCEAN

ATLANTIC OCEAN

Malindi

Mombasa

N

W E

S

Mozambique

Kilometers
0   1000   2000
Miles
0   1000   2000

Cape of Good Hope

From the beginning, da Gama charted a bold course. Instead of hugging the coastline of Africa, he headed straight out into the Atlantic, thousands of miles from land. Da Gama wanted to avoid the storms that often blow off Africa's coast. He also hoped the strong ocean winds would push his ships around the tip of Africa.

For three long months, da Gama's men saw only endless waves. Some of the crew panicked. Would the captain's risky plan work? Finally, on November 4, 1497, they spotted land! They anchored their ships in a bay north of the Cape of Good Hope.

Around Africa

Da Gama's fleet rounded the Cape of Good Hope and sailed up the eastern coast of Africa. The Portuguese stopped briefly at Mozambique. The Muslims there treated them well, but only because they thought the Portuguese were Muslims too.

By the middle of April, The Portuguese reached the Muslim city of Mombasa. The **sultan**, the Muslim ruler there, sent friendly greetings to the Portuguese. Da Gama learned that the sultan only wanted to lure the ships into the harbor so he could capture them!

A Portuguese fort at Mombasa

Boats like those da Gama saw on the Indian Ocean

A little farther up the coast, the fleet stopped at another Muslim city, Malindi. Malindi's sultan agreed to help da Gama with his voyage. The sultan thought the Portuguese might help him. He supplied them with food.

The sultan also ordered fragrant cloves, cumin, ginger, nutmeg, and pepper to be loaded onto the ships. He provided skilled pilots to guide the Portuguese across the Indian Ocean. Da Gama was very pleased, but wondered how long would his luck hold?

A handful of nutmegs

India At Last!

With the help of the pilots from Malindi, da Gama's fleet was able to cross the Indian Ocean in only 23 days. On May 20, 1498, the ships entered the Indian port of Calicut. The first people da Gama met in India were Muslim merchants.

The merchants were angry to learn that the Portuguese were in search of spices. They weren't going to let anyone take their business away. The merchants warned the Indians not to help these newcomers.

Da Gama went to meet Calicut's ruler. The king was not a Muslim. He was a **Hindu**, a believer in the traditional religion of India. The king didn't want to anger the Muslim merchants with whom he did a lot of business. So he allowed da Gama to buy food in Calicut, but nothing else. Da Gama sailed to other ports in India looking for people who might be willing to trade, but he didn't find any.

Da Gama decided to return to Portugal. Now the Indian Ocean's seasonal winds were blowing in the wrong direction. The trip back to Africa took over three months. The ships soon ran out of food and fresh water.

Many of the men developed **scurvy**, a deadly disease caused by a lack of vitamin C. By the time they reached the African coast in January 1499, more than 30 men had died. The men regained their strength in Africa and then set sail for Portugal. Da Gama vowed to return. When he came back the next time, he wouldn't accept failure—no matter what!

◄ Da Gama greets the ruler of Calicut.

Across Cultures

Da Gama's men thought the Hindus of Calicut were Christians. The Portuguese saw statues of Hindu gods, like the one above. The sailors thought the statues were of Christian saints and were puzzled by how they looked. "Their saints have teeth that stick out an inch from the mouth, and they have four or five arms."

War Over Trade

The fleet reached Portugal in August 1499, 26 months after it had left. Despite da Gama's failure to trade for spices in India, the voyage was seen as a huge success. Da Gama was given a hero's welcome. He wanted to sail back to India right away, but first he had to recover from the hardships of the voyage.

In 1502, da Gama returned to India. This time he had a fleet of 20 well-armed ships. Portugal was now determined to get even with the Muslims. As the ships approached Calicut, da Gama had his men set fire to a Muslim ship, killing everyone on board.

Da Gama also seized a group of fishermen in the harbor and hanged them from the masts of their ships. From then on, Portugal and the Muslims were at war in the Indian Ocean.

Sailors knew they had returned home safely when they saw Belem Tower in Lisbon's harbor.

A Muslim artist painted this sea fight with the Portuguese in the Indian Ocean.

It was a violent, bloody time. Da Gama spread terror wherever he went. The Portuguese now took control of the spice trade. They learned that most of the spices were not grown in India. They came from the Spice Islands in the Indies, thousands of miles to the east. The explorer Ferdinand Magellan would soon begin a search for a new route to the Spice Islands.

Chapter 3

Ferdinand Magellan

As a young man, Ferdinand Magellan joined Portugal's fleets that sailed to India after Vasco da Gama's historic voyage. Magellan longed to sail to the Spice Islands as captain of his own ship. The king of Portugal refused his requests.

Magellan went to the king of Spain with an idea. Magellan believed he could reach the Indies by sailing west around South America instead of east around Africa. The Spanish king agreed to support Magellan's voyage. But was such a long trip possible?

The fleet of Magellan (left) leaving Spain

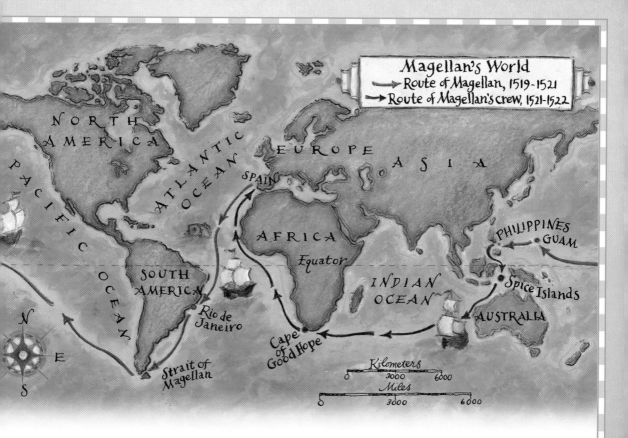

Magellan's World
→ Route of Magellan, 1519-1521
→ Route of Magellan's crew, 1521-1522

NORTH AMERICA

EUROPE

ASIA

PACIFIC OCEAN

ATLANTIC OCEAN

SPAIN

AFRICA

Equator

PHILIPPINES
• GUAM

SOUTH AMERICA

Rio de Janeiro

INDIAN OCEAN

• Spice Islands

AUSTRALIA

Cape of Good Hope

Strait of Magellan

N
E
S

Kilometers
0   3000   6000
Miles
0   3000   6000

Magellan had five ships and 250 men. The ships carried supplies for two years at sea. On September 20, 1519, Magellan's fleet sailed from Spain. Magellan's men were mostly Spanish. They didn't trust their Portuguese-born commander. Magellan didn't tell them that he planned to sail around the world. They probably wouldn't have agreed to sail with him had they known!

On December 13, the ships reached the coast of South America. No one was sure if there was a way to get to the other side of the continent. Magellan had heard stories about a **strait,** or passage, somewhere near its southern tip. He told his crew they would be heading south to look for the strait. The men were afraid. The seas were getting rougher and rougher. Where was Magellan leading them? And for what purpose?

The Westward Passage

As they sailed south, Magellan's Spanish crew grew more fearful. Magellan refused to answer questions about the voyage. The fleet neared the tip of South America as winter was coming on. Magellan knew they'd have to wait for better weather before they tried to continue.

The angry crew set up camp for the winter. They were farther south than any European had ever been. They found strange creatures, such as penguins and llamas. They also reported meeting giant people. Magellan called them "Patagones" because of their big feet. The area became known as "Patagonia."

It's a Mystery

In April 1520, a Spanish captain led a **mutiny** against Magellan. He promised the men to return to Spain. Magellan stopped the revolt and had the captain killed.

Finally, the ships left their winter camp and continued their search for the strait. Magellan examined every channel, every bay, every river, thinking it might be a westward passage. During this time, one of the ships deserted and sailed back to Spain.

It took months for Magellan to find a channel that looked like it might go through. The trip down this twisting passage was terrible! The sailors were sure they would die. On November 27, 1520, the fleet finally reached the other side of the continent. Magellan stared out at the Pacific Ocean and broke down in tears. Today, this passage is called the Strait of Magellan.

The Patagonian Giants

An Italian named Antonio Pigafetta sailed with Magellan. He claimed he met a Patagonian who was "so tall that our heads hardly came up to his belt." Later visitors to this area also reported meeting huge people. An English ship stopped there in 1765, but was unable to find any trace of the giants.

Magellanic penguins found on the coast of Argentina

Across the Pacific

Magellan had found a passage to the Pacific Ocean. Now he looked forward to reaching the Indies, but where were they? Week after week passed on the open sea, and still no land was spotted. Magellan's men grew sick from hunger and scurvy.

What little food they had left was rotten and covered with worms. The starving men had to eat rats to stay alive. On March 6, 1521, the ships finally reached the island that would later be known as Guam. The crew was able to get some much-needed fresh food. Little by little, their health was restored.

The island of Guam

Ten days later, the fleet reached another group of islands. Were these the Indies? At first, Magellan thought so, but he was wrong. These were the islands later known as the Philippines. The ships anchored at the first small island. Magellan sent a landing party to shore. The people were friendly, and they wore lots of gold jewelry.

Magellan decided to explore the other islands and look for the source of the gold. On April 7, the fleet reached the island of Cebu. Cebu's ruler asked Magellan to help him attack the nearby island of Mactan. The explorer agreed.

On April 27, Magellan and 60 of his men waded ashore at Mactan. The islanders attacked them with arrows, spears, and other weapons. Magellan ordered his men back to the boats. As he made his way through the water, he was struck by an arrow and killed. His body was never found.

Across Cultures

Lapulapu was the ruler of Mactan who defeated and killed Magellan. Today, Lapulapu is honored as the Philippines' first national hero. This statue of Lapulapu stands in a city named for him.

Around the World

After Magellan's death, his captains struggled for power. Finally, Juan Sebastian del Cano was elected the new leader. Many of the men wanted to return to Spain, but del Cano decided to continue west. No one dreamed it would take six more months to reach the Spice Islands.

In November 1521, the fleet finally reached the place Magellan had dreamed about years earlier. The men loaded up their ships with valuable spices. Only two of the original ships remained. One of them tried to sail home but was captured by the Portuguese. The Spanish crew was imprisoned.

Magellan's flagship, *Victoria*

Sebastian del Cano

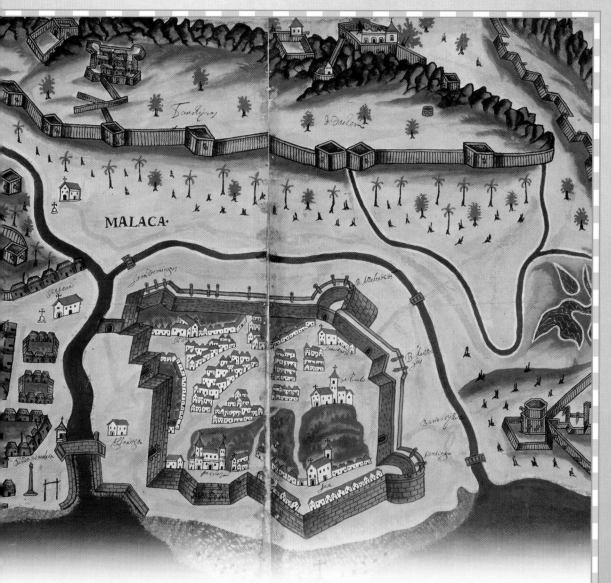

MALACA.

Old map of a port in the spice trade

The other ship, *Victoria*, made it across the Indian Ocean, around the Cape of Good Hope, and back to Spain. On September 16, 1522, nearly three years after Magellan set sail, *Victoria* reached home.

Only a handful of the original crew had survived to stagger ashore. These men had achieved what many had believed to be impossible. They had sailed around the world!

The World in the 1520s

The voyages of exploration begun by Prince Henry gave people of the 1520s a much truer picture of the world. The explorers who followed da Gama and Magellan had better maps, better ships, and better navigation tools.

By the 1520s, Portugal had become one of the most powerful countries in the world. But Portugal's time as a world power would not last.

Other European countries wanted their share of the riches that Portugal had found overseas. These countries struggled to claim their own **colonies** in many parts of the world. Much of this struggle was driven by greed. The worst result of this greed was the cruel slave trade that brought untold misery to countless Africans.

Imagination and a spirit of adventure also drove the explorers of this time. The greatest work of Portuguese literature is a long poem about Portugal's voyages to the Indies. The poet says of the Portuguese explorers, "If there had been more of the world, they would have found it."

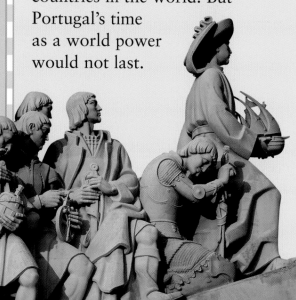

Prince Henry stands at the head of a long line of explorers in Lisbon's Monument to the Discoveries.

Glossary

caravel a small ship with several lateen sails

carrack a larger version of the caravel, with both lateen and square sails

colony an area ruled by another country

Hindu a believer in the traditional religion of India

Indies an old name for lands in Asia that were the source of valuable spices

lateen a three-sided sail

Muslim a believer in Islam, the religion founded by Muhammad

mutiny a revolt on a ship

navigator a person skilled at plotting a ship's course

Near East the region of southwest Asia that borders Europe and Africa

scurvy a disease caused by lack of vitamin C

strait a narrow passage between two bodies of water

sultan a Muslim ruler

A caravel pictured on a plate

Index